Oh Holy Night

Santa La Noche   Cantique de Noël

Princess Eli

by Ekaette Eli Shammah

 **Princess Eli**

Book Series

You are reading from the Princess Eli multi-lingual book series.

Princess Eli is a singing princess, who uses her songs to leave her stamp on the world. She loves singing in different languages and learning with her friends.

About the Author

Ekaette Eli Shammah is the performing artist known as Princess Eli. She sings, plays the ukulele, and is the author and illustrator of the Princess Eli book series. She holds a Bachelor's degree from Rice University and a MBA from the University of Houston Victoria. She loves working with children to make learning fun.

www.PrincessEli.com

Princess Eli

Song History

Oh Holy Night was written in 1843 in French as a poem by Placide Cappeau and was entitled Cantique de Noël. In 1847 Adolphe Adams composed the music for the poem, making it into the well-known Christmas carol we know today.

Oh Holy Night is a well-known Christmas carol that brings joy and warmth to the holiday season.

Princess Eli features the song Oh Holy Night in her multi-lingual book that is written in English, Spanish and French.

Characters

Princess Eli

Dutchess

Sir

Countess

Lady

Marquess

For Parents

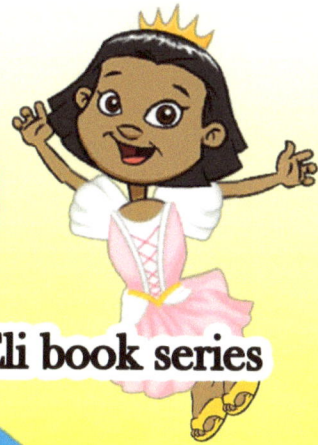

Tips for parents when reading the Princess Eli book series

Read the story with your child.

Get help pronouncing the words correctly by viewing the interactive videos at www.PrincessEli.com.

Sing the song with your child to aid in memorization.

Review vocabulary by asking your child if they know what each word means.

Princess Eli

 **Princess Eli**

Free Downloads

Pronouncing each word is as simple as pressing play.
Download the song in English, Spanish, and French,
and follow along with the story.
Visit PrincessEli.com/Free for your free MP3
that you can play from your phone, tablet, or laptop.

English

Español

Français

www.PrincessEli.com/Free

Princess Eli

Oh Holy Night

Santa La Noche

Cantique de Noël

Written and Illustrated by Ekaette Eli Shammah

Copyright 2016 Set on a Hill LLC
Houston, TX USA

www.PrincessEli.com

Oh holy night, the stars are brightly shining.

Santa la noche hermosas las estrellas.

Minuit, chrétiens, C'est l'heure solennelle.

I

It is the night of our dear Savior's birth.

La noche cuando nació el Señor.

Où l'Homme Dieu descendit jusqu'à nous.

Did you hear about the cat who swallowed a ball of yarn?

What happened to her?

L

Long lay the world in sin and error pining.

El mundo envuelto estuvo en sus querellas.

Pour effacer la tache originelle.

She had a litter of mittens.

Till He appeared and the soul felt it's worth.

Hasta que Dios nos mandó al Salvador.

Et de son père arrêter le courroux.

Why was the cat scared of the tree?

Why?

A thrill of hope the weary world rejoices.

Una esperanza todo el mundo siente.

Le mode entier tressaille d'espérance.

Because of its bark!

For yonder breaks a new and glorious morn.

La luz de un nuevo día al fin brillo.

En cette nuit qui lui donne un Sauveur.

What does a cat that lives near the beach have in common with Christmas?

What?

Fall on your knees! Oh, hear the angels' voices.

Hoy adorad a Cristo reverente.

Peuple à genoux, Attends ta délivrance!

Sandy claws!

Oh night divine! Oh night when Christ was born!

¡Oh, noche divina! ¡Nació el Salvador!

Noël! Noël! Voici le Rédempteur!

Oh night divine! Oh night when Christ was born!

¡Oh, noche divina! ¡Nació el Salvador!

Noël! Noël! Voici le Rédempteur!

Cat-alogues!

Princess Eli

Fun Club

Join the fan club today and download for free the MP3 audio story in English, Spanish and French!

The fan club features fun activities, coloring sheets, the chance to win concert tickets, and the latest cat jokes!

Follow Princess Eli

www.instagram.com/PrincessEliMusic

www.facebook.com/PrincessEliMusic

www.PrincessEli.com

www.ingramcontent.com/pod-product-compliance
Lightning Source LLC
Chambersburg PA
CBHW040023050426

42452CB00002B/110